Countries and Cultures for Young Explorers

KENYA

Written by
Lynita Strei

Inside Illustrations by
Sherry Neidigh

Cover Illustration by
Laura Zarrin

Publisher

Instructional Fair • TS Denison
Grand Rapids, Michigan 49544

About the Author

Lynita Strei has a degree in Cultural Studies and Comparative Literature from the University of Minnesota. She has edited and done research for other educational texts. This is her first adventure with authorship. Lynita enjoys playing, learning, and exploring with her ten nieces and nephews and her 3 1/2-year-old daughter, Josephine, who hopes to be a world traveler someday.

Credits

Author: Lynita Strei
Illustrator: Sherry Neidigh
Cover Artist: Laura Zarrin
Cover Graphics: Peggy Jackson
Project Director/Editor: Sara Bierling
Editors: Mary Hassinger, Linda Triemstra
Page Layout: Tracy L. Wesorick

Standard Book Number: 0-7424-0033-6
Countries and Cultures for Young Explorers: Kenya

a Division of Instructional Fair Group, Inc.
a Tribune Education Company
3195 Wilson Dr. NW
Grand Rapids, Michigan 49544

Table of Contents

Introduction

Kenya is a country rich in culture and beauty. Young students will explore this colorful and diverse land through activities and information intended to spark their imaginations.

A young resident of Kenya named Joseph guides students along the journey by providing narratives from a child's point of view. Students will learn about Joseph's home, family, favorite meals, and games as they hear personal stories that vividly portray Kenya's culture with fun and excitement. Sections narrated by Joseph are identified by a picture of Joseph near the beginning of each narrative. These stories provide background material for the activities, but may be long for reading aloud in single sittings. We suggest you read Joseph's information in parts, as needed or appropriate. Use your best judgment as to what will captivate your students' attention. Those sections not narrated by Joseph are best read by the teacher and the information given to the students as needed.

Accompanying each narrative is a set of activities, varying from discussions to projects, from which the teacher may choose. Many activities may be made easier to suit younger students.

Included are cross-curricular activities and projects, reproducible pages, and minibooks. These pages are designed to actively involve the students in learning about the cultures of Kenya. Many student worksheets apply directly to the activities presented in the teacher pages. Others are simply supplementary and may be completed by students on individual bases.

Students begin the adventure through Kenya with a reproducible flag and passport. The students may color the flag and fold the passport. To make passports more authentic, students may draw pictures of themselves or paste in photos.

A traveler's suitcase pattern is included at the back of the book to allow students to save the worksheets and projects they have completed. This will not only help students retain learned information but also remind them of the fun and adventure they experienced during their study of Kenya.

Utilize the resource lists in the back of the book to enhance your trip with Kenyan music, photographs of featured subjects, children's books about Kenya, and educational Web sites.

Have fun with your adventures!

Kenya

Passport

Citizen of Kenya

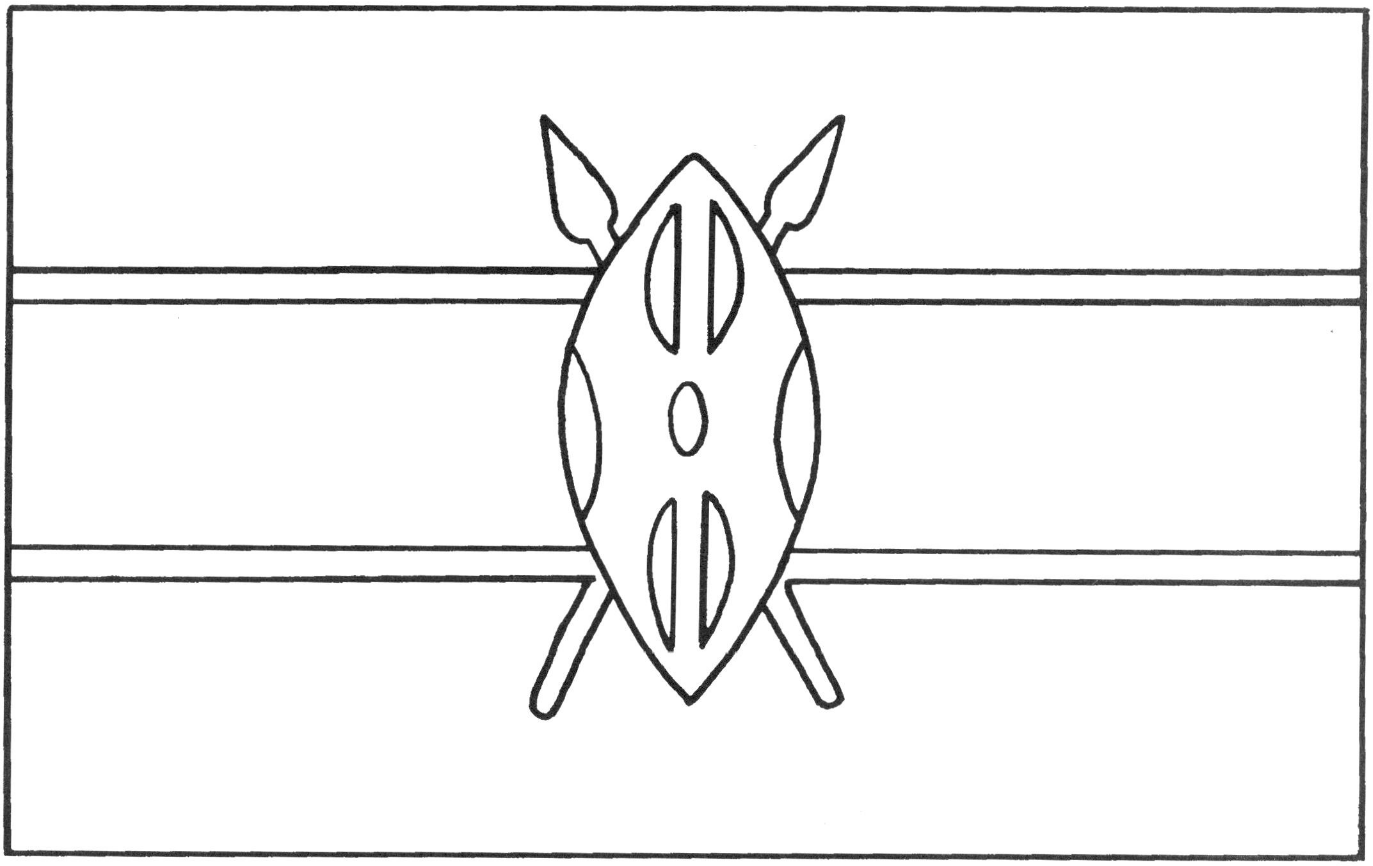

Jambo!

Jambo (JAHM-boh)! That is how we say hello in *Swahili* (swah-HEE-lee), the national language of Kenya. My name is Joseph, and I live in Kenya. Kenya is in East Africa.

My people are called *Masai* (mah-SIGH). We live in the savannas in the southwest of Kenya. We call it Masailand. There are green, rolling hills that lead up to the highest mountain peak in Africa, *Mount Kilimanjaro* (kil-i-mon-JAH-roe). The mountain is actually in the country of Tanzania, but it is called the center of Masailand.

My mother, father, older brother, and I live in a Masai village called a *kraal* (KRAHL). There are twelve huts in our kraal, surrounded by a fence of thorn bush. The thorn bush is as sharp as barbed wire and keeps out wild animals, such as lions, rhinoceroses, and elephants, as well as cow thieves.

The Masai people have raised cows for hundreds of years. I began learning how to care for them when I was a small boy—only three or four years old. They are very important to us as a source of nutrition, and we get to know each cow as if it is our friend. Sometimes we even sing to our cows.

My mother built our hut. It is shaped like a dome and is made of branches, twigs, and grass. Our house does not have lights or windows. It is perfect to keep us warm and dry when the rainy season comes.

Activity

For information on Kenya, go to *http://sbwm.erols.com/pmnet/jambo/home.htm* on the Web.

Activity

Use the chart on page 8 to help students chart their family life.

Activity

Reproduce the mini-book on page 9 for students to color and read. Help students complete the word search on page 10.

Activity

Create a mural of a Masai village. Paint a large piece of poster board or a paper-covered bulletin board with savanna grasses. Include a watering hole, some dome-shaped mud huts, and mountains in the distance. Have the students make animals and figures to add to the mural. Be sure to include thorn-bush fencing, cows grazing, a stalking lion or leopard, hippos in the watering hole, Joseph with a long spear and wearing a red toga, a herd of elephants, a rhinoceros, sheep, and goats.

Blue Jeans or Togas

Many people like my family still live in the traditional way they have for hundreds of years. There are only two big cities in all of Kenya. Sometimes people become tired of living in the kraal and want to find jobs in the city to make more money. They send money home to their families to make life on the savanna easier. I think it would be strange living in a tall apartment building with busy streets and cars all over. Life on the savanna is hard work. I have many chores, but I would miss roaming with the cattle on the open grasslands and playing hide-and-seek with my friends in the kraal.

The Masai have become more modern in some ways. For example, some of my people wear blue jeans instead of the traditional red toga. A toga is a long cloth wrapped around the waist and over the shoulder.

Another tradition we no longer have, because of Kenya's laws, is the lion hunt. My people are great warriors. In the past, a boy would have to kill a lion all on his own. This proved he was a brave warrior. The best warriors would wear real lion's mane headdresses. Sometimes I wish we still practiced the lion hunt, but then I think that saving the animals is better.

The great warriors of the Masai are called *moran* (moh-RAN). I hope to be a moran someday. My friend, Lekorrio, and I practice our bravery with a game that we play. We place small rocks on a sleeping rhinoceros. The last one to place a rock on the rhinoceros's back before it wakes up is the winner. Last time Lekorrio won, so I plan to challenge him to another game. This game is very dangerous. A rhinoceros has a large horn and can weigh up to 4 and a half tons!

My older brother Kureko is almost fifteen. Fifteen is the age at which he will have to leave the kraal and live out in the bush with other young men. It is very dangerous. There are lions and leopards. Kureko wants to be a moran because he knows that it would make my father very proud. But, he does not want to miss school. Kureko knows that without an education he could not become a teacher. He hopes to move to the city someday and teach at a private school. I do not know if I would ever want to leave Masailand. For now, I know that I must go to school to learn what I can.

Activity

Discuss: Would students have the courage to go on a lion hunt? Ask them why they think it is important not to hunt lions anymore.

Activity

Play the rhino game. One student should get on his or her hands and knees on the floor and be blindfolded. The other students stand in line to place small pieces of paper or dried beans on the student's back. The last one to place a piece before the student moves is the winner.

Dress Up Kenyan Style

Many Kenyans have adopted western styles of dress, even in the country. But many women still wear colorful *kangas*. Kangas are pieces of fabric usually about 5 by 3 feet (1.5 x 1 m). They are worn as skirts, as shawls, or over the head. Mothers also use them to carry their babies.

Jewelry is worn by both men and women in Kenya. Beautifully beaded necklaces, earrings, and bracelets are common. Each group has its own unique style. Some jewelry symbolizes wealth or status. During celebrations and festivals, many people dress up with extra-special jewelry as well as headdresses and masks.

Activity

If possible, bring in large pieces of fabric (old sheets work well) for the students to try wearing in different ways. They may wrap them around their heads or waists. Or, research culture groups in Kenya and find pictures of the different styles of dress. Have students note the colors and patterns in the fabrics.

Activity

Have the students experiment with making African necklaces. If beads are not available, try using different kinds of pasta. The pasta can be dyed by mixing 1 tablespoon (15 ml) vinegar, some food coloring, and 1 cup (240 ml) hot water. Soak the pasta in the dye for a few minutes, let dry, then string into unique patterns. Try on your kanga with your new, colorful jewelry!

Activity

Help students sort the culture cards on page 11.

House and Home

My House

Parents	**Made of**
Kids	**How many windows?**
Pets	**How many doors?**

1 My name is Joseph. I live in a Masai kraal.

2 My mother built our hut.

3 We put up thorn bush fences to protect us.

4 I love being on the savanna.

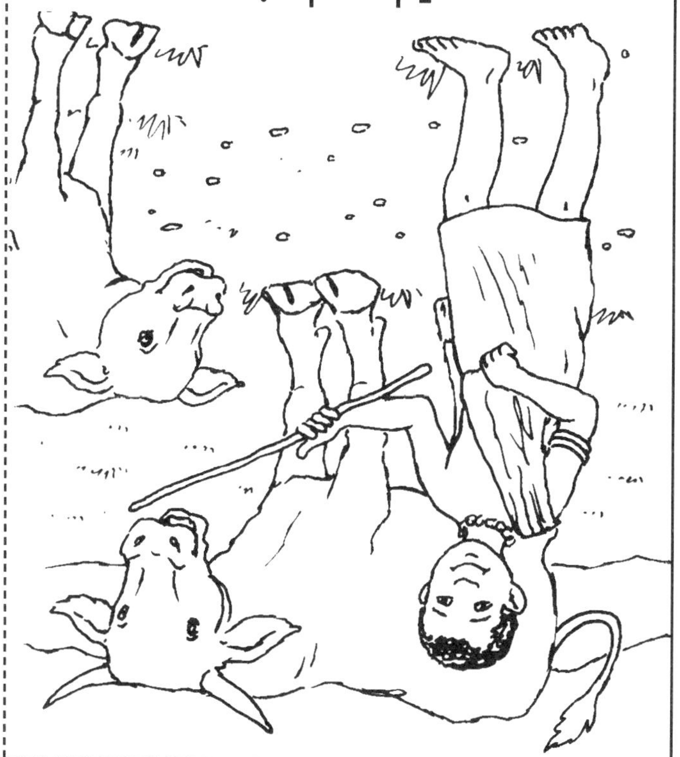

Savanna Search

Find these words that relate to Joseph's life on the savanna. Cross out each word in the word search as you find it.

Word List

lion
sheep
hut
goat
cattle
snake
bird

Challenging Words

jambo
Masai
Kenya
herd
kraal
savanna

s	n	a	k	e	b	g	c
a	l	b	i	r	d	o	e
m	p	k	e	n	y	a	d
h	e	r	d	f	h	t	m
u	s	a	v	a	n	n	a
t	j	a	m	b	o	s	s
v	r	l	i	o	n	h	a
c	a	t	t	l	e	e	i
q	g	o	u	i	t	e	j
x	s	z	k	c	w	p	n

Mombasa or Masailand

Color and cut out these pictures of African life. Divide the pictures into two piles, one for traditional items and the other for modern items.

Cultures of Kenya

The Masai

Joseph's family belongs to the Masai culture group. The Masai have traditionally herded cattle. But, they were also known as fierce warriors. The Masai have always been nomadic people, but more of them are now settling in permanent homes. The Masai are only one of the many groups of people that live in Kenya.

Activity

Read *Masai and I* by Virginia Kroll. This children's book compares a modern little girl's life to that of a Masai.

The Kikuyu

The Kikuyu people are farmers and live in mud houses like the Masai, but their houses are larger and have thatched roofs. They also raise cattle and sheep. They can grow coffee where they live in the highlands in the middle of Kenya. One of Kenya's most famous leaders, Jomo Kenyatta, was Kikuyu. Kikuyu people value their traditions, but also enjoy many modern conveniences. Kikuyu is the largest culture group in Kenya.

Activity

Have students draw pictures of a Kikuyu village. Items included could be huts with thatched roofs, grassy hills, coffee plants, and cattle and sheep.

The Luo

The Luo mainly live in large fishing villages on the shores of *Lake Victoria*, which is the largest lake in all of Africa and the second largest freshwater lake in the world. They fish with boats called *dhows* (DOWS). These small sailboats, with beautiful white sails, have been used in Kenya for hundreds of years. The fish the Luo catch are sold at markets or shipped to Nairobi, the capital of Kenya. The Luo also farm corn, rice, and millet for food. Many Luo also live in the cities of Kenya and are skilled craftsmen.

Activity

Help each student make a dhow (wooden fishing boat). Fold a piece of brown construction paper lengthwise, gathering the ends so that the paper forms a vessel. Use a drinking straw for a mast by inserting it through a small hole in the bottom of the boat and taping in place. Make a triangle-shaped sail out of white paper and attach to the top of the straw with tape.

Activity

Rumor has it that a giant serpent lives in Lake Victoria. Have students create serpents using geometric paper shapes of varying colors. Make sure they use a repeating pattern. After they have laid out their patterns, have students glue them to sheets of paper and add eyes and long tongues.

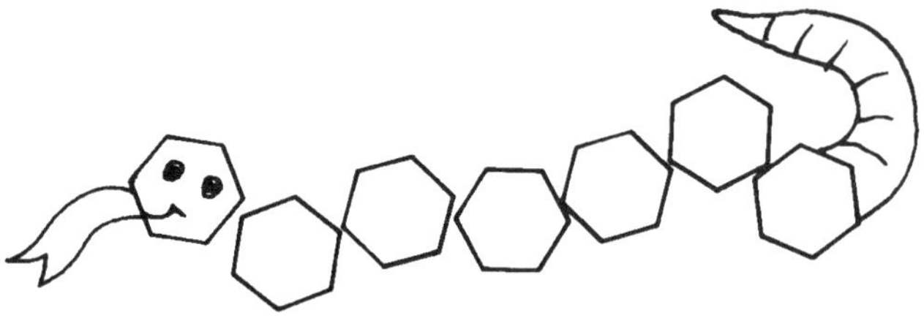

The Turkana

The Turkana people live near another big lake in Kenya called *Lake Turkana*. They herd cattle, like the Masai, and have very little contact with the modern world. Even though Lake Turkana is large, it is in the middle of a land that is extremely dry. There is very little rainfall and the weather is very hot most of the year. The Turkana cannot grow food because of the heat and lack of water. They use the lake to catch fish in nets. They even eat the crocodiles that roam the waters.

Activity

Have the students help make sugar cookies shaped like crocodiles and decorate with green sugar. Then the students will be able to eat crocodiles, too!

Or, make crocodiles out of toothpaste boxes. A second box cut in half and split open can serve as the jaws.

The Samburu

The Samburu live in the surrounding highlands of Lake Turkana. They are fortunate to live in a green paradise, compared with the sandy, desertlike land of their neighbors, the Turkana. Samburu land is alive with tall grasses, meadows, and green cedar trees. There is plenty of rainfall, and they are able to grow food. They also raise cattle. They believe that friendship is more important than money or property.

Activity

The Samburu are very friendly people. Have students brainstorm ways to make their classroom more friendly. Include a discussion of how to make new friends. Present these ideas on a poster or classroom bulletin board.

Activity

Have students color and read the minibook on page 14.

Activity

Help students fill in the chart on page 15 with characteristics of each tribe mentioned in the narratives above. Younger students may draw pictures illustrating characteristics.

Traditional Ceremonies

The Masai have their own festivals and celebrations, as do the other groups in Kenya. A wedding or the birth of a baby is cause for a huge celebration. Joseph and his family dress in their best togas and finest jewelry for these ceremonies. The dances of the Masai moran are shows of amazing athletic skill. The dancers jump so high off the ground they seem to wear springs! The men wear headdresses of feathers and soft lion's mane. The women wear brightly-colored kangas, and everyone wears hundreds of colorful beads.

Another special time for the people in southwestern Kenya is in April. This marks the start of the rainy season. They move their cattle to fresh grassy fields with overflowing streams of water. They pray for healthy cattle and abundant grazing lands.

Activity

Have a jumping contest! In the spirit of the Masai moran, see how high each student can jump. Have a panel of students judge the winner.

Activity

Many groups of people in Kenya have their own style of headdress. Usually they are made of things in their environment that are important to them, like ostrich feathers and lion's mane.

Have students design headdresses. They should draw pictures of themselves wearing African headdresses. If possible, collect real feathers or other items to add to the picture.

1 Kikuyu people grow coffee.

4 The Samburu believe that friendship is very important.

2 The Luo people fish in Lake Victoria.

3 The Turkana live where it is dry and hot.

Culture Chart

Kikuyu	Luo

Samburu	Turkana

Education and Language

Harambee Schools

Many schools in Kenya are run by private organizations that want Kenya's children to get a good education. The government cannot afford to educate every child in Kenya. People work together so that we can all go to school.

Not very long ago, there were no schools for my people. We relied on the elders to teach us the skills we needed to be Masai—raising cows, building houses, and living on the savanna. Today, we have schools where we learn reading, writing, science, geography, Swahili, and even English. I am glad that we have schools, even though sometimes I would rather be sitting on the savanna with the cows than doing my math homework.

At school, we sing the national anthem. Before starting class, it is our job to clean the school. We have to mop the floors, empty the trash, clean off the blackboard, and weed the school's garden. Our school cannot afford to pay someone to clean it for us. Sometimes I do not feel like helping with these chores, but then I remember how lucky I am to have a school.

At lunch time, we eat the soup or porridge that has been cooking in the big pot on the fire all morning. Sometimes we bring vegetables from home to add to the potatoes, carrots, corn, and beans in the soup. We sit outside with our bowls and eat in the shade.

In Kenya, paper, books, and other school supplies cost a lot of money. We have to share books and desks. We write on scraps of paper or chalkboards instead of notebooks.

Activity

Many schools in Kenya are started by people who want the children to get a good education. As a class, brainstorm a list of things that someone would need to start a school. Why are these things important?

Activity

At the beginning of the school day, have students help you tidy up the classroom. They should also water any classroom plants and feed classroom pets.

Activity

Cook a pot of lunch-time soup for your students. Use a crockpot or hot plate to cook a simple soup using root vegetables that you or your students bring in.

Activity

Have students color and read the mini-book on page 18.

Activity

Students may help Joseph get to school by guiding him through the maze on page 19.

Speaking Swahili

jambo (JAHM-bo)—hello

kwaheri (kwah-HAY-ree)—goodbye

karibu (kah-REE-boo)—welcome

la (LAH)—no

naam (nah-AHM)—yes

samahani (sah-ma-HAH-nee)—sorry

asante (ah-SAHN-teh)—thanks

harambee (hah-RAHM-bay)—let's all pull together

Activity

Practice these new Swahili words by having each student choose one or two words to say to the class.

Activity

Read this book to practice more Swahili words: *Jambo Means Hello: Swahili Alphabet Book* by Muriel Feelings.

Count to Ten

moja (MO-ja)—one

mbili (em-BEE-lee)—two

tatu (TA-too)—three

nne (EN-nay)—four

tano (TAH-no)—five

sita (SEE-tah)—six

saba (SAH-bah)—seven

nane (NAH-nay)—eight

tisa (TEE-sah)—nine

kumi (KOO-mee)—ten

Activity

Practice pronouncing the numbers as a class. To help with this lesson, read *Moja Means One: Swahili Counting Book* by Muriel Feelings.

Activity

Use the number cards on page 20 to help students practice the numbers in Swahili. They can identify the number by reading the word or numeral, or by counting the objects on each card.

Activity

Help students complete the coloring activity on page 21.

Swahili Phrases

Habari gani? (ha-BAH-ree GAH-nee)—What's happening?

Nzuri. (en-ZUR-i)—Things are good.

Salama. (sa-LAHM-ah)—Everything is peaceful.

Tutaonan. (too-taoh-NAN)—We will see each other again.

Lala salama. (LA-la sa-LAHM-ah)—Sleep peacefully. Good night.

Asante sana. (as-SAHN-teh SAH-nah)—Thank you very much.

Manners

Hand and facial gestures are often used to express thoughts. In Kenya, people show approval with two thumbs up. Finger pointing is considered rude. To point something out, you would use all of the fingers of your right hand.

In Masailand, children are not to speak to an adult until they are spoken to first. This is one way they show respect for their elders. They must look down at the ground until they are touched on the head. A Masai mother rarely calls her children by their given names. She will usually call them "my eyes" or "my legs" in an affectionate tone.

Activity

Learn to speak Swahili on the Internet! Go to *www.supersurf.com* and click on Kenya and then on "Fun from Afar."

1 We sing the Kenyan national anthem.

2 It is the students' job to keep our school clean.

3 Math is NOT my favorite subject.

4 Lunch time!

Kraal Crawl

Joseph walks to school everyday. Can you help him find his way out of the kraal and through town to his school?

moja 1
mbili 2
tatu 3
nne 4
tano 5
sita 6
saba 7
nane 8
tisa 9
kumi 10

Coloring Cows

1 = red	2 = blue	3 = yellow	4 = purple	5 = green
6 = orange	7 = brown	8 = black	9 = white	10 = pink

Kenyan Playtime

Although many Kenyans cannot afford to buy fancy toys like action figures and video games, the children find plenty to do. Joseph likes to play soccer with his friends and his brother. Soccer is a very popular game all over Kenya. They do not have fancy equipment. Usually they use wrapped-up rags for a ball and a tree as a goal post.

Mancala is a board game played with seeds or pebbles. It is a complex game in which pebbles are moved through a series of spaces to "capture" the other player's pieces. The game can be played without a board simply by making wells or divets in the dirt and collecting some pebbles.

It is expensive to buy books and even paper in Kenya. So, instead of reading, storytelling is very popular all around Kenya. Kenyans tell stories to pass on family history, to teach children how to behave, and for fun.

Activity

Organize a soccer game. Have students improvise by coming up with nonstandard objects for the goals and the ball (e.g., two trees and wadded-up rags).

Activity

Make your own mancala game. Many children in Kenya have to create games and toys out of objects they have handy. Follow these instructions to make a simplified version of mancala.

Materials:

cardboard egg carton
two small cups (paper or foam)
48 pebbles of similar or equal size
scissors
tempera paints (optional)
glue

Directions:

1. Cut the lid off the egg carton.
2. Glue the bottom inside the lid.
3. Paint if desired.

Object:

To collect the most stones in the mancalas (these are the small paper cups).

Set Up:

1. Place 4 stones in each of the egg cups. Do not place stones in the mancalas. Mancalas go on either end of the long board.

How to Play:

1. Each player "owns" the mancala to his right and the six small cups on his side of the board.

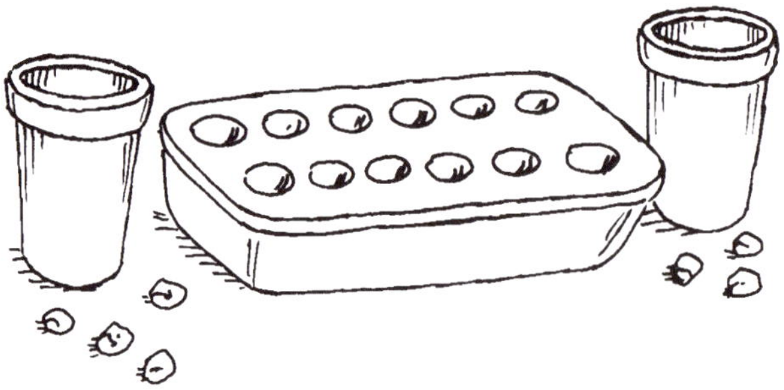

2. Player A starts by taking all the stones from any one of his small bowls.
3. Player A drops one stone into the next bowl on the right, one stone into the second bowl on the right, continuing around the board (counterclockwise) until he has no more stones in hand.
4. If player A reaches his own mancala, he drops a stone into it. If the stone is his last, he gets to move again.
5. If the player drops his last stone into one of the empty bowls on his side of the board, he may keep that stone, plus all the stones in the opponent's bowl directly opposite. He then places them in his mancala.
6. The game ends when one player no

longer has stones in his cups. The other player (who still has stones on his side) places all remaining stones into his mancala.

NOTE: If this seems too complicated for younger students, see if they can create their own game with the supplies listed.

Activity

Have a storytelling day! Ask your students to relate stories or details about a class trip or experience. Have them raise their hands and give suggestions that you write on the the chalkboard or on poster paper. Or, each student could write one sentence or draw one picture about a certain event. These pages could be compiled and bound as a classroom book.

Activity

Dancing is a popular form of recreation in Kenya. Play some music for your students and let them dance creatively. Or, you may wish to structure the dance period by giving them a set choreography to follow. Another option is to instruct the students to dance by imitating the movements of some African animals, such as elephants or baboons.

Olympic Games

Kenyans may not have fancy sports equipment, but many great athletes have come from Kenya. Kenya is very proud of its talented long-distance runners. Living in this rough land and not having a car to travel everywhere is great training for Olympic runners.

There was one special Olympic athlete who is still an inspiration to Kenyans. His name is Kipchoge Keino. He grew up living in a mud hut, much like Joseph's, and herded goats and cattle.

In 1968, Kip went to the Olympics in Mexico City. He really wanted to make Kenyans proud. Even though he was very sick at the time, he won a gold and a silver medal! He went on to win more medals and break several Olympic records. Kip is still considered a hero today.

Activity

Have students decorate and cut out the plaque on page 24. They can be displayed on a bulletin board highlighting the achievements of Kipchoge Keino.

Activity

Have the students run a set distance each day for a week. Time how long it takes them to run the course. Use the chart on page 25 to record the times and set goals. Give out awards for each goal accomplished. Use stickers or stars to denote success.

Train Like Kip

Ahmed	***3.54***	★
Sara	***3.00***	★
Kureko	***3.43***	
Julio	***3.50***	
Brian	***3.00***	
Maria	***4.00***	★
Alyson	***3.87***	
Brett	***4.01***	
Meredith	***2.98***	
Rashell	***3.35***	★
Matt	***3.22***	

Honorary Plaque

Decorate this plaque to honor Kip Keino.

Train Like Kip

Student Name	Date/Time	Date/Time	Date/Time	Date/Time

Kenyan Holidays

Kenya was once a colony of England. That means it was run by the British government. Because of this, many Kenyans celebrate Easter, Christmas, and other Christian holidays.

Native Kenyans did not like being ruled by others who did not know their traditions and ways of life. They fought hard to run their own country. Finally, on December 12, 1963, Kenya became an independent nation. Their first president was Jomo Kenyatta. He was called *mzee* (EM-zay), meaning "wise one." He was the leader who thought of the motto "Harambee!" which means, "Let's all pull together!" He would get huge groups of Kenyans all chanting "Harambee!! Harambee!!" to excite the people into working as a united country.

Jamhuri Day (Independence Day) is held every December 12. People gather for traditional dances, choir performances, and presentations by school children. The day is finished with an evening soccer game.

Kenya's first free president is honored on another day, *Kenyatta Day*, October 20. There are parades, and the people listen to speeches given by government leaders. Then there are elaborate traditional dances. School children might sing with a choir or march with their class in the parade. There may be soccer games and other contests, and then, of course, a huge feast.

Activity

Have students color and read the mini-book on page 28.

Activity

Celebrate Kenyan independence by writing a poem about the country. Use the acrostic form on page 29 and choose words to describe Kenya that begin with each letter in the word K-E-N-Y-A. For example:

Kikuyu
Elephants
Nature
Youthful
Africa

Activity

See the flag of Kenya and read the national anthem on the World Wide Web at *www.rcbowen.com/kenya/anthem.html.*

Activity

Use the flag template on page 30 and have students create their own flag. Explain to them that the three colored bars on the Kenyan flag stand for the Kenyan people, the struggle for independence, and agriculture, respectively (black = people, red = independence, green = agriculture). The shield and spears stand for the defense of freedom. Have the students think about what's important to them and then decorate the flag accordingly. Every student should explain to the class what each component of their flag means.

Play to the Beat

Kenyan music can be heard at every celebration, holiday, festival, and religious ceremony. The drum is the most common instrument. The drum plays the pounding beat, a flute or stringed instrument plays another rhythm, and there is usually a chanting or singing part. This music is the driving force behind many spirited gatherings in Kenya.

Music can also be heard pouring from the shops in Nairobi. Kenyans listen to rock, disco, jazz, soul, hip-hop, rhythm and blues, reggae, and Western classical, as well as modern music from some of the different tribal groups.

There are many songs that are written for animals. Joseph sings to his cattle. Other people have special songs they sing for the animals that provide them with food, clothing, and transportation.

Activity

Learn more about Kenyan music on the World Wide Web at *www.africaonline.com/AfricaOnline/music/kenya.html.*

Activity

Borrow drums and flutes from your school's music department or make your own drums. Have each student bring a coffee can or oatmeal box to make a drum. Have the students decorate their drums. They can play different rhythms at the same time. Or, you may wish to play recordings of African music. Some suggestions are *Missa Luba* and *Holding Up Half the Sky: Voices of African Women.*

Classroom Festival Day

Kenyans celebrate in many different ways. Some paint their bodies with symbolic designs; others have prayer ceremonies or rituals. Most all of the festivals in Kenya involve dancing, music, singing, and eating.

To make your classroom festival authentic, do some of the following:

Mask: Reproduce the mask pattern on page 31 and have students color and cut out. The masks may be attached to tag board or poster board or used as is. Use strings stapled to each side to tie masks around the students' heads.

Dancing: Research African dances and learn one as a class. Have the students dance while you play a simple rhythm on one of the homemade African drums.

Shield: African shields are often used symbolically in dance rituals. Have each student make his or her own African shield and hold it while dancing. Use a large plastic lid or cardboard cut-out circle and cover it with colorful construction paper. Make geometric designs with different colors of paper to create a unique pattern. Then, make four holes in the shield with scissors—one on either side at the top and one on either side at the bottom. Thread string through the holes and crisscross to make a handle in the back of your shield.

Face Painting: This is an activity all children love. Put an African twist on it by researching designs—geometric patterns, animals—that are unique to Africa.

African Dress: Have the students bring in a "kanga" to wear for the event. This could be a sheet, blanket, or old tablecloth—the more colorful the better! The students should also wear their homemade jewelry (from page 7).

Storytelling: This is a Kenyan tradition. Many folktales focus on animals and nature. Read a Kenyan folktale about an animal. Some suggestions are *The Lonely Lioness and the Ostrich Chicks: A Masai Tale* retold by Verna Aardema and *Rabbit Makes a Monkey of Lion: A Swahili Tale,* also by Verna Aardema.

Have the students come up with their own folktale about the existence of some animal with which they are familiar. They may write or draw their story in a mini-book.

Kenyan Food: Serve Kenyan food using the recipes in the following section. Also, try to bring in some fruits native to Kenya such as oranges, bananas, plantains, and dates.

1 Kenyatta Day is celebrated on October 20.

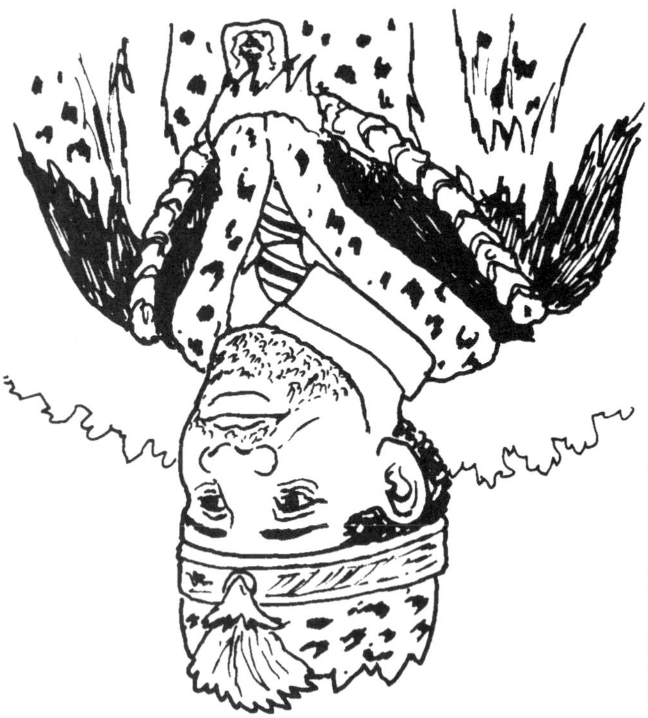

4 Music is played all day.

2 Everyone shouts "Harambee! Harambee!"

3 Kureko jumps the highest!

K ______________________

E ______________________

N ______________________

Y ______________________

A ______________________

Mask Pattern

Eating in Kenya

The types of foods eaten in Kenya are as diverse as its people. The Masai get much of their nutritional needs met from the cattle they raise. However, they do not eat meat very often. Meat is only for special meals. They drink cows' milk, and sometimes mix it with the cows' blood. Cow's blood provides a strengthening protein to the Masai diet. The blood is taken from the cow by inserting a blunt arrow into its neck. Then the hole is packed with mud and cow dung until more blood is needed. Like many Kenyans, the Masai also eat bread, potatoes, and corn that they buy in local stores.

Throughout Kenya ugali is eaten. *Ugali* is similar to mashed potatoes but made from cornmeal. It is a thick porridge often eaten with vegetables or beans.

A popular drink is called *chai*. It is tea sweetened with lots of sugar and milk. This is such a tasty drink that it is becoming popular all over the world.

Bread is made in many different ways around Kenya. One of the most common kinds of bread is called *chapati* (cha-PAH-tee). It is a fried bread that was brought to Kenya by the Arabs.

There are many fruits native to Kenya. Dates, figs, pineapples, bananas, and plantains are all eaten in Kenya. Plantains are kind of like bananas. Bananas and plantains are eaten fresh or roasted, fried, baked, or steamed. The Kenyans have creative ways of preparing many of their fruits.

Activity

Look up more Kenyan recipes on the Web at *www.rcbowen.com/kenya/recipes*.

Activity

Fry bananas. Cut several bananas into two or three pieces each. Coat each piece with beaten egg and then with flour. Deep fry in very hot oil until golden. These are delicious with vanilla ice cream.

Activity

Make chai for your students. Boil 3 cups (720 ml) of water, 4 decaffeinated tea bags, 6 cardamom pods (cut in half), 3 to 6 thin slices of fresh gingerroot, and 6 teaspoons (30 ml) of sugar for about 10 to 20 minutes. Do not allow to boil dry. Remove the tea bags. Add 3 cups (720 ml) of milk to the pot and bring to a boil again, being careful not to scald the milk. To serve, strain over a mug. This recipe will serve 6 to 7 students.

Activity

Bring in native Kenyan fruits for your students to sample. Bananas, pineapple, tangerines, oranges, dates, figs, and coconut are all excellent examples.

Activity

Lead students to notice that none of the recipes in their study of Kenya contain meat. The Kenyan diet is primarily composed of vegetables. The Masai get their protein from cow's blood—the Turkana from crocodile meat—but many other groups do not get much protein at all. Explain to the students that healthy human beings need to get foods from each of the food groups every day. Draw a chart on the chalkboard similar to the one below. Have students give examples, from their breakfasts and lunches, of foods that go in each group. Explain to students that we need different amounts of foods from each group (e.g., small amounts of fats, oils, and sweets). Have students evaluate whether they have eaten well on that day.

Kenyan Words to Learn

ugali (oo-GAH-lee)—cornmeal porridge

chai (CHAI)—sweetened tea

chapati (cha-PAH-tee)—fried flat bread

plantain (plan-TANE)—banana-like fruit

Recipes to Try

Fufu

Ingredients:
- 3 cups (720 ml) sweet potatoes (cooked and mashed)
- 1/2 cup (120 ml) fine bread crumbs
- 1 tsp. (5 ml) salt

Directions:

1. Combine all ingredients together in a large bowl.
2. Cook in a skillet over low heat for about 10 minutes, stirring constantly.

Banana Boats (Banana Dhows)

Ingredients:
- 1 banana per student
- 1 tbs. (15 ml) shaved coconut per student
- whipped cream
- toothpicks, or craft sticks cut in half—one per student
- white paper

Directions:

1. Have students prepare the sails for their boats. Cut a small, triangular sail out of the white paper—of a size proportional to the toothpick or piece of craft stick. They should then tape the sail to the mast.
2. Give each student newspaper to lay on his or her desk. Each student should have one banana (peel on)—with a small bit of the top cut out, like a cap—1 tbs. (15 ml) coconut, a spoon, his or her sail, and a small bowl for mashing.
3. Students should scoop the banana out of the peel and mash it in a bowl with the coconut. After the mixture is thoroughly mashed together, they should spoon it back into the peel, which is the body of the boat. (For younger students, you may wish to prepare the boats ahead of time or mash the banana and coconut for them.
4. Give each student a small dollop of whipped cream on top. Each student should insert their sail and enjoy!

Recipes

Mango Snow

Ingredients:

4 unripe mangoes, peeled and thinly sliced
2 tbs. (30 ml) sugar

Directions:

1. In a pot with just enough water to cover the bottom, steam the mango slices until soft. Make sure the water doesn't boil away, because the mangoes may stick to the bottom of the pot.
2. In a blender or food processor, combine the mangoes and sugar and blend until smooth. Or, mash with a potato masher until all of the lumps are gone.
3. Serve immediately or chill. Serves 6. Variation: Mix 1 cup (240 ml) of whipped heavy cream into the chilled mango purée.

Ugali

Ingredients:

1 cup (240 ml) cold water
1 cup (240 ml) yellow cornmeal
1 tsp. (5 ml) salt
3 cups (720 ml) boiling water

Directions:

1. Mix the cold water, cornmeal, and salt in a saucepan. Bring to a boil over high heat.
2. Add the boiling water.
3. Mix until smooth.
4. Simmer over medium heat for about 10 minutes, stirring frequently.
5. Serve hot and eat carefully with fingers.

Recipes

Chapati Bread

Ingredients:

2 cups (480 ml) flour
1 tsp. (5 ml) salt
oil (or butter, melted)
water

Directions:

1. Sift the flour and salt into a bowl.
2. Add enough water to make a stiff dough.
3. Roll the dough onto a floured board and make a thick circle.
4. Brush with oil or butter. Knead. Repeat this 2 or 3 times.
5. Divide the dough into four or five balls and roll out into flat circles.
6. Heat a frying pan over medium heat and brush with oil.
7. Fry each piece of chapati until golden brown on both sides. Serves 4.

Ugali is often eaten with a dish called *Sukuma Wiki*. This means "stretch the week" in Swahili. It is called that because it is an inexpensive meal and will get you through the week.

Sukuma Wiki

Ingredients:

6 cups (1,440 ml) chopped kale or collard greens
3 tbs. (45 ml) vegetable oil
1 onion, chopped
1 cup (240 ml) chopped tomatoes
1/2 cup (120 ml) water
salt and pepper

Directions:

1. Heat the oil in a large skillet.
2. Sauté the onion.
3. Add the greens, tomatoes, and water.
4. Cook covered, on low heat, until the greens are softened.
5. Add salt and pepper to taste. Serve with chapati bread or ugali.

Animal Safari

People from all over the world go to Kenya to see its amazing animals. Imagine sitting in a comfortable hotel eating breakfast and gazing at a water hole where hippopotamuses, zebras, and giraffes are quietly drinking. Tourists provide more money for the people of Kenya than everything except the sale of coffee and tea. Kenyan safaris are world famous.

The animals roam free and happy in the protected lands in Kenya where hunting is prohibited. There are huge herds of wildebeest, antelope, zebras, and African buffalo. Other plant eaters found in smaller groups are giraffes, hippos, rhinoceroses, and elephants. Elephants are Kenya's largest mammals. An adult elephant can weigh more than 12,000 pounds (5,400 kg) and stand more than ten feet (3 m) tall.

Meat eaters lurking in the tall grasses include cheetahs, leopards, jaguars, hyenas, and lions. These prey on the plant eaters. Cheetahs are the fastest land mammals in the world. They can reach speeds of 70 miles (113 km) per hour!

There are many monkeys and baboons that fill the trees of Kenya. They have been known to venture into towns and villages raiding vegetable gardens. How would you like to chase a blue-faced baboon out of your garden?

One of the most spectacular sights in Kenya is the giant flocks of flamingos that cover the large lakes. They look like enormous pink clouds floating above the waters.

The ostrich is another famous African bird. Ostriches cannot fly but can run up to 40 miles (64 km) per hour.

Snakes of all kinds live in Kenya. They are rarely seen, though. They sense the vibrations of a person walking on the ground and slither to their underground holes before being spotted. Pythons are among the world's largest snakes and can grow up to 30 feet (9 m) long. Their thick bodies wrap around their victims and strangle them to death! Most of the time, however, people are not in danger from pythons.

Activity

Have students color and read the minibook on page 38.

Activity

Read *Why Mosquitoes Buzz in People's Ears* by Verna Aardema, a version of a classic African folktale. How many different animals are mentioned or pictured?

Activity

How many students would it take to equal the weight of one African elephant? Weigh the students in your class and find out!

Activity

Help students complete the cheetah flicker book on page 39 to see how fast a cheetah runs.

- Cut along all solid lines.
- Put the picture cards in order 1–10 and staple together on the left edge.
- Flip the book pages to see how the cheetah runs.

Activity

Reproduce the patterns on page 40 for each student. Students can color and cut out. The limbs and tail of the monkey can be attached using brads. Students may add textual details, such as plastic eyes, fabric, and colored cotton balls.

Activity

Measure 30 feet (9 m) with chalk on the floor of the classroom or outside. See how many students fit into the length of one python, laying head to foot.

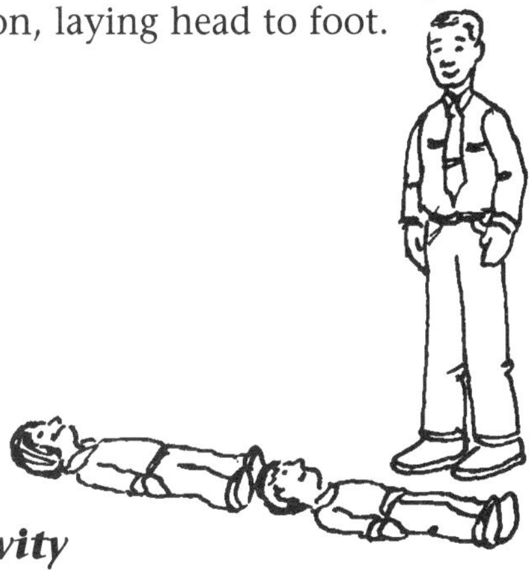

Activity

Explore Kenya's wildlife on the Internet. To see pictures of Kenyan wildlife and hear a trumpeting elephant and the screeches of a monkey, go to *http://sbwm.erols.com/pmnet/kenya/wildlife.htm* or to *http://sbwm.erols.com/pmnet/jambo/fauna/wildlife.htm.*

Activity

Contact Kenya's wildlife service and see what they are doing to protect and preserve animal habitats.

Web site address:
www.kenya-wildlife-service.org

e-mail address: *kws@kws.org*

mailing address:

The Director—
Kenya Wildlife Service
P.O. Box 40241
Nairobi, Kenya

Telephone: (254-02)501 081/2

fax: (254-02)504171

Activity

Have students color and cut out the animal cards on page 41 to use as flashcards to learn Swahili words. Or, students may use the cards to make adjective books. They should staple the pages together at the left to make a small book. Each student should think of one or two adjectives for each animal and write them on the pages. Explain to them that adjectives describe nouns by telling about color, number, size, shape, feel, smell, etc. As a class, share the adjectives and keep a list on the chalkboard or add to a word wall.

Activity

Have students brainstorm careers that deal with animals (e.g., vet, zoologist, park ranger, pet groomer, animal breeder, taxidermist, marine biologist, poacher, dog walker, animal trainer, horse racer). Pick several from your list and ask students to supply some requirements of the jobs. Would any of the students like to have these careers?

Activity

Obtain several copies of *National Geographic* magazine. Have students cut out pictures of Kenyan (or African) animals (you may wish to provide a list on the chalkboard). After the class has gathered enough pictures, you can create an animal collage on a classroom bulletin board.

Activity

Ask the students: Would any of these Kenyan animals make good pets? Why or why not? Follow this up by asking students if they think these animals rely on humans in any way.

1 Tourists let the animals come to them.

4 Baboons raid vegetable gardens.

2 Elephants have the right of way.

3 Cheetahs can run very fast!

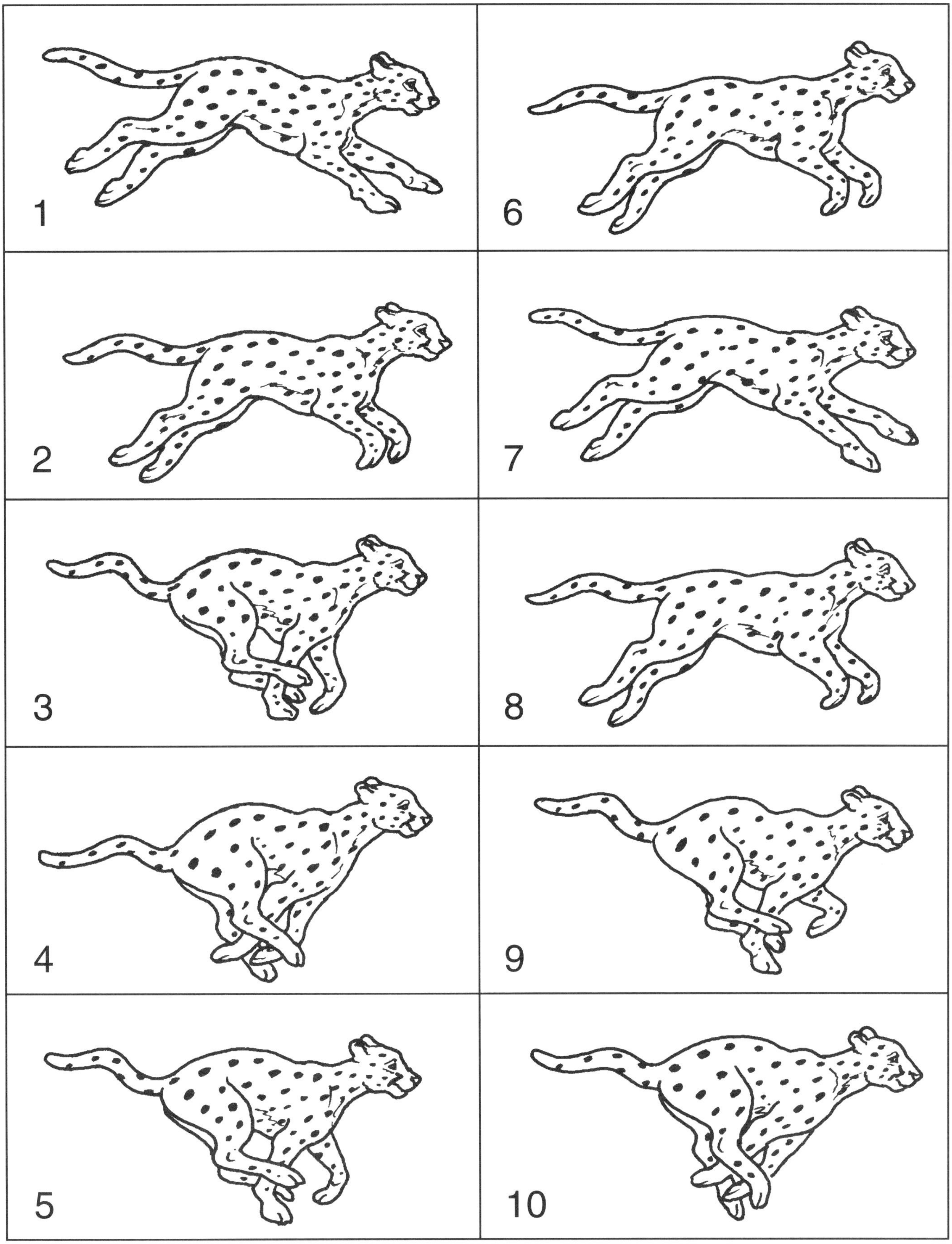
1
6
2
7
3
8
4
9
5
10

Monkey Patterns

Swahili Animal Names

elephant — tembo

hyena — fisi

buffalo — mbogo

ostrich — mbuni

lion — simba

wildebeest — nyumbu

Digging Up the Past

The Great Rift Valley in Kenya is sometimes called the "Cradle of Humankind." This is not because it is shaped like a cradle but because it is the place many anthropologists believe the first humans were born. Some of the oldest skulls and bones in the world have been found there. People were living in this valley of Kenya more than one million years ago. We do not know much about these people because they left no written records.

Louis and Mary Leakey, two anthropologists, uncovered hundreds of fossils in the valley. They discovered bones and two-million-year-old tools. When Mary Leakey was done putting the bones together, she had discovered a very old human skull.

Fossils are things like bones or leaves that become hardened or leave an imprint in soil. Over time, the soil becomes hardened rock. Mary Leakey found human footprints someone left behind about one million years ago. Scientists like the Leakeys can understand many things about these ancient people just by looking at a footprint.

Activity

Have your students make their own fossil imprints. Have them pretend they are anthropologists studying fossils.

Materials:
- self-hardening clay
- bones, shells, leaves, or small tools

Directions:

1. Make balls of clay and then flatten out.
2. Press shells, bones, leaves, and other items into the clay. Then remove the items.
3. Allow the clay to dry.
4. Have the students test their classmates to see if they can guess what item made each fossil.

Activity

Reproduce page 44 for each student. Have the students match the fossil imprint with the object that made it.

Activity

Create a classroom dig. Get a large tub (a plastic storage tub would work well). Fill the tub about half full with soil or sand. Place a number of items at different levels in the soil. Have the students carefully uncover the treasures using spoons. Provide a worksheet similar to the one pictured below on which students can list each item where they found it—the top, middle, or bottom of the tub (younger students may draw the items).

Top	skull, arow
Middle	bone
Bottom	shell, tool

Activity

Have students draw pictures of what they think life was like during the time of early man.

Geography

Kenya is a little smaller than the state of Texas in the United States. The equator runs straight through the country. Crossing the equator is the Great Rift Valley. This is like a huge gash in the earth's surface. Many of Kenya's people live in the highlands on either side of this valley. They have rich soil for growing crops and comfortable temperatures. Plains and rolling grasslands with thorny trees and bushes spread out from beyond the highlands.

Most of the national parks in Kenya are in the south. The biggest of these is Tsavo National Park. Kenya's eastern border is 300 miles (483 km) of tropical white sand beaches along the Indian Ocean. This area is lush with mangrove trees and coconut palms. It is a popular tourist destination.

There are two large cities in Kenya. One of them is on the coast and is called *Mombasa*. Mombasa began as an Arab trading post. The other city is the capital of Kenya. It is called *Nairobi*. This city got its name from the Masai word meaning "place of sweet waters," because it was where the Masai used to bring their livestock to graze and drink water. The water hole is no longer there. Nairobi is now a modern city with tall skyscrapers, movie theaters, restaurants, hotels, and busy streets. Lions, elephants, and giraffes can be seen in their natural habitats just a few miles from the city's center.

Activity

Help students complete the map activity on page 45.

Activity

Have students study a detailed map of Kenya. Then have them add details to the map on page 45, such as a compass, mountains, wildlife sanctuaries, bodies of water, etc.

Activity

Reproduce the map on page 45 for a third time. Explain to the students that there are three types of land in Kenya—tropical coast, dry plains, and fertile highlands. As a class, decide where each region is in Kenya. Have students mark their maps with different colors to designate these areas.

Activity

Lake Victoria, in the southwest corner of Kenya, was discovered in 1858 to be the source of the Nile River. A British explorer, John Speake, traveled through Africa until he finally found it. Have students imagine they are trying to find the source of the Nile. They should draw a picture or write a story about their expedition.

Activity

See Nairobi from a bird's eye view. Go to *www.rcbowen.com/kenya/cities/nairobi.html* on the Web and click on "Nairobi" for a closer look.

Activity

Find out what the weather is like today in Kenya. Either look it up in a newspaper weather section or find out on the Internet (*www.weather.com*).

Activity

Explain to your students that Kenya is in the continent of Africa. Show them a map of Africa and point out how many different countries there are. Then ask the students to list some words that describe Africa. After their response, explain that, just like the state or province where they live, Kenya has similarities and differences from other African countries (e.g., dress, food, climate, traditions).

Activity

Invite someone who has traveled to Kenya to speak to the class. Ask them to bring photographs, slides, or souvenirs from their trip. After the visit, ask the students what they would most like to do on a trip to Kenya.

Activity

Have students write stories about an African adventure. They could work with partners to create the stories, or the class could give ideas as a whole. Make sure they add colorful drawings to their creations.

Fossil Find

Draw a line to match the fossil imprint with the object that made it.

Map Activity

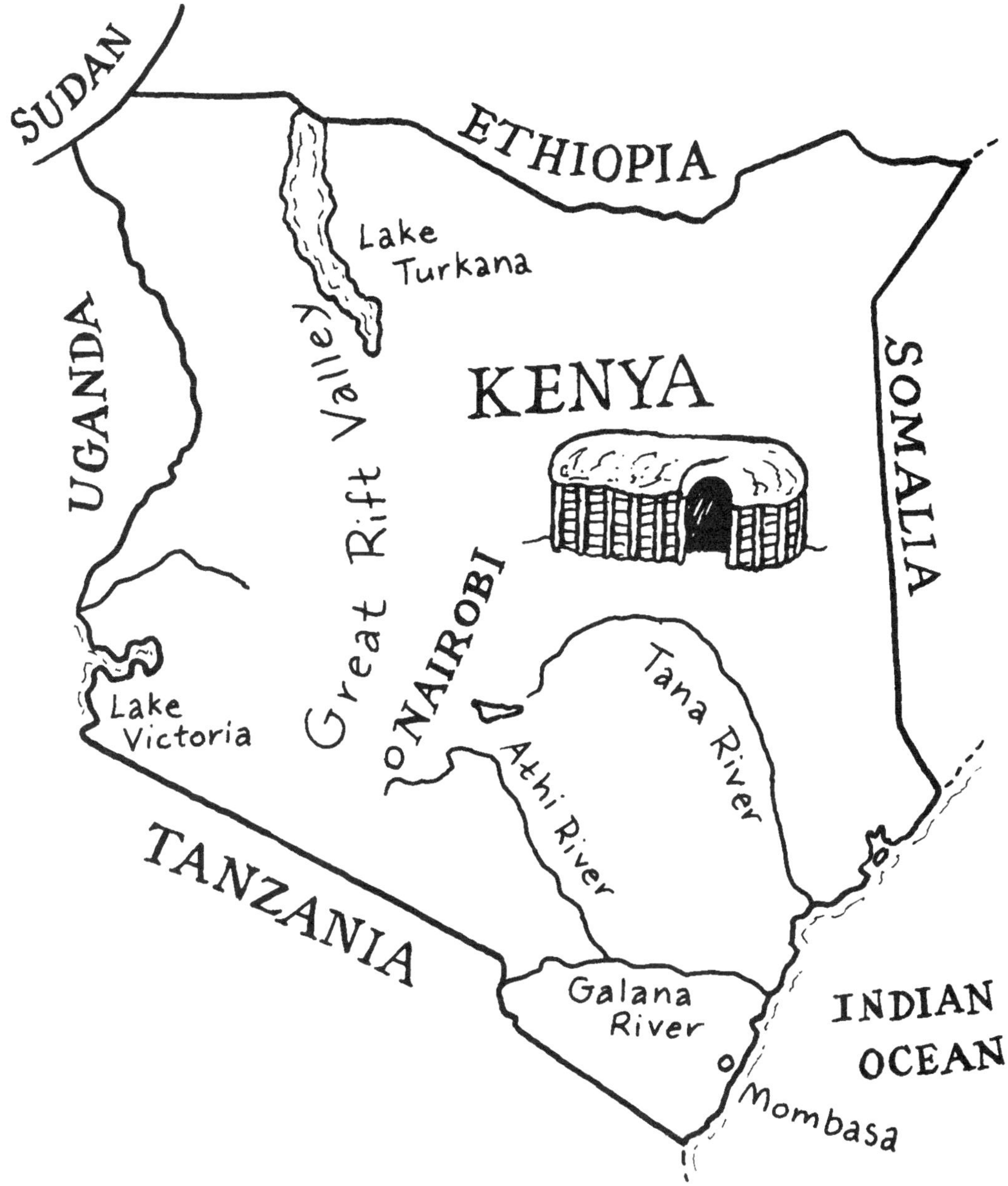

1. Draw a wooden sailboat in the Indian Ocean.
2. Color the Great Rift Valley brown.
3. Draw a blue star where Nairobi is marked.
4. Color the dome-shaped hut red.
5. Color Lake Turkana and Lake Victoria blue.

Instructions:
Enlarge to 200%. Fold on the dotted line. Then glue the sides of the suitcase, leaving the top open. (You may wish to glue the suitcase to a file folder for added stability.) Punch out the circles with a hole punch and thread yarn or string through the holes. Knot the thread for handles.

References

Bibliography and Photographic Reference

Buettner, Dan. *Africatrek: A Journey by Bicycle Through Africa*. Minneapolis: Lerner Publications Company, 1997.

Burch, Joann J. *Kenya: Africa's Tamed Wilderness*. Parsippany, NJ: Dillon Press, 1997.

Hetfield, Jamie. *The Maasai of East Africa*. New York: PowerKids Press, 1996.

King, David C. *Exploring Cultures of the World: Kenya: One Nation, Many Cultures*. New York: Benchmark Books, 1998.

Lands and People. Volume 1. Danbury, CN: Grolier Inc., 1997.

Pateman, Robert. *Cultures of the World: Kenya*. New York: Marshall Cavendish, 1993.

Shachtman, Tom. *Growing Up Masai*. New York: Macmillan Publishing Co., Inc., 1981.

Stein, R. Conrad. *Enchantment of the World: Kenya*. Chicago: Children's Press, 1985.

Zeleza, Tiyambe. *Maasai*. New York: The Rosen Publishing Group, Inc., 1994.

Children's Literature Reference

Aardema, Verna. *Bringing the Rain to Kapiti Plain: A Nandi Tale*. New York: Dial Press, 1981.

—*The Lonely Lioness and the Ostrich Chicks: A Masai Tale*. New York: Alfred A. Knopf, 1996.

—*Rabbit Makes a Monkey of Lion: A Swahili Tale*. New York: Dial Books for Young Readers, 1989.

—*Why Mosquitoes Buzz in People's Ears: A West African Tale*. New York: Dial Press, 1975.

—*Who's in Rabbit's House?: A Masai Tale*. New York: Dial Press, 1977.

Feelings, Muriel L. *Jambo Means Hello: Swahili Alphabet Book*. New York: Dial Press, 1974.

—*Moja Means One: Swahili Counting Book*. New York: Dial Press, 1971.

Kroll, Virginia. *Masai and I*. New York: Four Winds Press, 1992.

Mollel, Tololwa M. *Big Boy*. New York: Clarion Books, 1995.

—*The Orphan Boy*. New York: Clarion Books, 1990.

Musical Reference

Holding Up Half the Sky: Voices of African Women. Shanachie, 1997.

Missa Luba. Muungano National Choir. Uni/Philips, 1991.

References

Web Site Reference

(The date in parentheses represents the last date the Web site was checked by the publisher.)

Jambo!

Jambo Kenya, Homepage, <http://sbwm.erols.com/pmnet/jambo/home.htm> (21 February, 2000).

Education and Language

Global Internet Attitude Co., Homepage, <http://www.supersurf.com> (21 February, 2000).

Kenyan Holidays

Africa Online, Inc., "Music," <http://www.africaonline.com/AfricaOnline/music/kenya.html> (21 February, 2000).

"Kenya's Flag & National Anthem," <http://rcbowen.com/kenya/anthem.html> (21 February, 2000).

Eating in Kenya

"Kenya–Recipes," <http://www.rcbowen.com/kenya/recipes> (21 February, 2000).

Animal Safari

Kenya Online, "East African Wildlife," <http://sbwm.erols.com/pmnet/kenya/wildlife.htm> (21 February, 2000).

Jambo Kenya, "Wildlife," <http://sbwm.erols.com/pmnet/jambo/fauna/wildlife.htm> (21 February, 2000).

Kenya Wildlife Service, Homepage, <http://www.kenya-wildlife-service.org> (21 February, 2000).

Digging Up the Past

"Nairobi," <http://www.rcbowen.com/kenya/cities/nairobi.html> (21 February, 2000).

The Weather Channel Enterprises, Inc., Homepage, <www.weather.com> (21 February, 2000).